AMISH WOMEN

AMISH WOMEN

LIVES and STORIES

LOUISE STOLTZFUS

Good Books

Intercourse, PA 17534

Acknowledgments

Illustrations on the front and back covers, pages 4, 30, 47, 70, 83, 96, 119
by Florence Starr Taylor. Copyright © 1986.
All rights reserved. Used by permission.

Design by Dawn J. Ranck

AMISH WOMEN
© 1994 by Good Books, Intercourse, PA 17534
International Standard Book Number: 1-56148-129-7
Library of Congress Catalog Card Number: 94-34166

Library of Congress Cataloging-in-Publication Data

Stoltzfus, Louise, 1952-
  Amish women : lives and stories / Louise Stoltzfus.
    p. cm.
   1. Amish women--Pennsylvania--Lancaster County. 2. Lancaster County (Pa.)--
Social life and customs. 3. Lancaster County (Pa.)--Biography. I. Title.
F157.L2S77 1994
305.48'687--dc20
                         94-34166
                          CIP

Table of Contents

I Was Once Amish

I was once Amish. Sometimes it seems I should say, "I am still Amish." For I have found it impossible to separate my life as an Amish person from my life as a late twentieth-century career woman. I am like the women who nurtured me. The values of my mother and my grandmothers still inform my decisions and my choices. They probably always will. I cannot escape who I am. I am schooled in the ways of the Amish.

I enjoy plain things.

The warmth of an Amish kitchen.

The smell of farms in early spring.

The fall harvest of gardens and fields.

The feelings of family and home.

Sometimes I long to sit in a quiet house lit by a gas lantern and spend an evening quilting or reading or talking with children. No television. No stereo. No telephone. None of the convenient distractions of the jet age.

Sometimes I even wonder what it would take for me to become Amish again. Could I give up these trappings of "the world"? Could I really go back to driving a horse and buggy? Could I think like an Amish woman? I doubt it, but still I wonder.

CHAPTER TWO

They Were My Grandmothers

Both of my grandmothers were Amish women born in Lancaster County in the last years of the nineteenth century. They married in 1911 and 1913 and lived quite similar, yet very different, lives.

My Grandmother Fannie came from a long line of strong women who took no nonsense from anyone. They made decisions. They married well. Some never married at all. They worked hard and loved and flourished and died.

My Grandmother Mary came from a line of weaker women. They were sometimes sickly and frustrated and occasionally even hopeless and depressed. But Grandmother Mary and the women who came after her took hope in one oft-repeated story.

Several generations before Grandmother Mary's time, a native American woman fell in love with her Amish neighbor, joined his church, and married him. According to legend, she was full of life and energy and brought spirit and hope to that particular

European Amish line. Grandmother Mary married into that family. It is said the native characteristics still appear in the dark features and burnished looks of many of the descendants of that woman.

"That's the reason for the wild blood," they all used to shake their heads and say.

◆　◆　◆

The Ebersol women from whom Grandmother Fannie came were anything but wild. They were staid and straight and sometimes even sour. They had orderly rows in their gardens. They religiously cleaned their houses upside down and inside out every spring and fall. They insisted on speaking pure German and corrected anyone who let the English-isms of Pennsylvania Dutch sneak into their late nineteenth-century language. No one pushed them around. But no one had much fun with them either.

It was said that when my great-grandmother Mary Ebersol Lapp married, she did not marry as well as her sisters would have liked. They did not approve of her husband-to-be or his lazy streak, as they called it. They would rather not marry than have him for a husband. But Great-Grandmother defied them and married anyway.

My Grandmother Fannie inherited some of both her mother's Ebersol austerity and her father's carefree Lapp love for life. She filled her kitchen, her children, and her grandchildren with homemade rootbeer floats, sandtarts, soda water, stewed crackers, turkey filling, fried oysters, eggs poached in milk, and mashed potatoes to die for. Her garden overflowed with fresh spring onions, radishes, turnips, and even an occasional exotic vegetable such as kohlrabi, for which we always pined during its long gestation period. She surrounded herself with rows of burgeoning grapevines, huckleberry bushes, and fruit trees. The weed-free flowers in her beds seemed to dance and laugh.

Grandmother Fannie also always found time to relax. Her father had taught her well. She rarely missed reading the "funnies" in the daily *Intelligencer Journal*. She invited tired grandchildren into her arms and held us close. She berated *Dawdy* (our name for Grandpa) for teasing the little ones and told on him everytime, assuring our skeptical, frightened eyes that there were no bogeymen down by the creek, but even so, we could not go down there alone to play.

She taught us to adore the great, old house in which she lived.

Where she was born.

Where she married.

Where she gave birth to nine children.

Where she died.

She let us slide down the magnificent open stairway banister. She watched us play hide-and-go-seek in her dimly lit warm rooms while she visited with Dad and Mom and all the other aunts and uncles. She punched holes in the tops of mayonnaise jars and laughed as we ran around her front yard on balmy summer evenings catching lightning bugs.

◆　◆　◆

Grandmother Fannie wore long, nondescript dresses of dark colors that folded around her slowly expanding, sagging, and aging frame. She pinned on her caps, capes, and aprons. Her hair slowly went from black to steel gray.

Always before we left—late at night, after dark, and when it was long past time for everyone to be in bed—she led us to the rolltop desk beside her bed where she hid her candy stash. The candy always softened the pain in our tearful eyes as we reluctantly left her side after spending another glorious day in her domain.

◆　◆　◆

Once in a great while, Grandmother Fannie could be coaxed to recount the story of her wedding day. December 14, 1911. She told of tables overflowing with the bounty of Amish life, friends gathered from throughout the Lancaster County Amish community, relatives who traveled from Ontario, and two precious, stolen moments on the staircase.

Grandmother's eyes always twinkled as she remembered coming around the sharp turn in the enclosed middle stairway of their house and finding herself alone with her new husband for the first time on that impossibly busy day. What did they do? She never would tell us.

She only smiled and said, "It was our first chance to be alone after we were married."

◆ ◆ ◆

Grandmother Fannie loved to work with her hands. After the house, farm, and yard work were done, she would sit in her favorite chair by the coal stove or on the front porch in the summertime and make straw hats. She had learned wheat weaving as a child and, in her Amish way, made useful things—hundreds of men's straw hats. Hats that my Amish brothers and their many cousins and friends slowly wore out.

Amish people from all over Lancaster County bought and wore Grandmother's hats. My brothers liked bright new ones for church. They wore them until the last tattered remnants without rims perched on their heads as they helped milk the cows. At the end, the hats always smelled of stables and sweat.

◆ ◆ ◆

Grandmother Fannie was a quintessential Amish woman of her time. She was a mother. She spent her days cleaning and sewing and cooking. She loved her husband—an Amish preacher—and dutifully filled her role as a preacher's wife.

The land was fertile, so she always had plenty of food and enough money to live comfortably. In fact, *well*, by Amish standards. She had lots of friends. She enjoyed hosting people, often entertaining overnight guests who arrived by train from the scattered Amish communities.

◆ ◆ ◆

Then came the morning when her son Christian collapsed in the tobacco field adjoining her home. Dead at age fifty-four with a heart attack. The tears streamed. The viewing spilled somberly into a once bright and happy place, and people wept silently with great gulps of grief. Christian's carefree twin teenage sons became the keepers of Grandmother's flame—the family farm—the home of her father and mother and grandfather and grandmother.

Dawdy was old. Christian was gone. And the only other men on the farm were teenagers, suddenly cast as men. They tried. They tried very hard. But the light was truly gone from the old home.

Dawdy died five long years later, and the house and yard were turned over to one now-married grandson's new wife.

At age ninety-six, Grandmother Fannie still worked in the garden. When she died in her one-hundredth year on earth, it seemed time stopped for those of us who loved and revered her. A way of life had ended.

This remarkable Amish woman, whose life spanned a century of change, had maintained a place full of stories, full of books, full of old furniture—a place of memories. A place that opened doors for her grandchildren, even as she marveled at their unpredictable lives.

"I don't see why you want to fly in the sky. Are you sure you will come back down?" she once asked me in complete concern, never mind the exasperation with which I received the question. She thought it all quite impractical.

◆　◆　◆

My Grandmother Mary was a more complex person. She married a man who found it difficult to make a living as a farmer. Not making a living at farming was not acceptable in the Amish community of the mid-1900s. Such a person, it was said, needed to learn to "be a better manager."

When Grandmother Mary was fifty-one, her husband died after a
long bout with cancer, leaving her and the children physically, but
never leaving them emotionally. Years after his death, she still
sometimes sank into depression and cried for her grown daughters
not to leave her house or her side.

We cried with her when she spoke with great longing about her
son who had moved far away. From the high cabinet came a book
about Alaska, displaying in striking color the landscape of the place
where Levi had gone. He wrote erratically and seldom visited,
eventually choosing not to come home at all.

These many years later, his story has risen to legend in family lore.
What we know is that he is a poet who lives alone and near poverty
in a large city. What many of us do not know or understand is how
he manages to survive without the family.

◆　◆　◆

Like her son, Grandmother Mary, too, was an artist. Her children
remember her sewing room retreat. There, she spent hours behind
a closed door, stitching quilts and braiding rag rugs which became
masterpieces of color, reflecting an inner life quite unlike the reality
of her everyday existence.

She was one of those turn-of-the-century women who created
what have become classic Amish quilts, combining deep purples,

greens, blues, reds, and blacks into bold patterns. Today these quilts are celebrated, not only for their unusual juxtaposition of color and design, but also for their display of artistic genius.

Some of the quilts and rugs which Grandmother Mary made now occasionally hang on museum walls. Others are lit by track lighting in the homes of her many middle-class, non-Amish grandchildren. Others are carefully folded and kept in chests and closets of other grandchildren, some of whom are still Amish.

Grandmother Mary would be quite surprised.

And quite pleased.

For she wove her love and faith into the fabrics of the pieces she gave her children and grandchildren, hoping we would use them for our deepest needs. We did. Many pieces were worn out. Some were saved. Others were sold to collectors of Amish antiques to provide much needed income.

◆　◆　◆

Grandmother Mary was a different kind of Amish woman, doing the best she could. People sometimes said her husband was strange. They moved from place to place, living in small, rental properties. When he died in 1940, Grandmother Mary was left with thirteen children, ages six to twenty-six, no money, and no home of her own.

Only rarely and with halting words of compassion and longing do Mary's children talk about their childhoods. They remember being cared for by neighbors whenever Mother was sick and sometimes spending weeks in strange houses which slowly became familiar and still bring quick, bright tears and sad, sure pain. They tell of living through the Depression with few worldly resources, of depending on the goodwill of family, neighbors, and friends. And of determining with iron grit and sure hope not to have such desperation, such loss of hope, or such pain repeated in their own lives.

◆ ◆ ◆

Both of my grandmothers' possessions have long since been parceled out. Many people hold different stories and portions of their lives. Occasionally an aunt or uncle or cousin shows a sturdy piece of furniture or pulls down a quilt from a closet shelf. Now quite out of context, the treasures are still called Grandmother Fannie's flour chest or her kitchen cupboard or Grandmother Mary's Center Diamond quilt or her Shooting Stars rug.

CHAPTER THREE

She Is My Mother

My mother is one of Grandmother Mary's fourteen children. Early in life she learned that the world is an alien place. A place sometimes of sadness. A place sometimes of pain. A place sometimes of parting.

She was only twelve years old when her father died. His fragile mental state, combined with cancer, made it impossible for him to participate in normal family life for most of my mother's growing-up years. What she remembers are his weekend visits home from the hospital.

In what Mom calls, "one of her last good memories," the family gathered around their kitchen table. That evening, as they sometimes did, they brought out the English hymnbooks and sang together.

Oh, how they sang!

"I can still see him standing there, singing that old hymn, 'There Were Ninety-and-Nine.' He had such a beautiful voice. Isn't it something that I remember him singing that song?"

"There were ninety-and-nine that safely lay,
"In the shelter of the fold,
"But one was out on the hills away,
"Far off from the gates of gold.

◆　◆　◆

"But the Shepherd made answer,
"This of mine has wandered away from me,
"And although the road be rough and steep,
"I go to the desert to find my sheep,
"I go to the desert to find my sheep."

It is such an atmosphere and consciousness that shaped my mother's childhood. Her understandings. And her world.

◆　◆　◆

My father is one of Grandmother Fannie's nine children. The coming of my father into my mother's life changed everything for my mother. They were married during an all-day Amish ceremony on November 22, 1951. The wedding was festive and happy.

They were in love.

The china sparkled.

The food was bountiful.

Several hundred friends and relatives sang and feasted and celebrated with them. It was a wonderful and joyous time.

My father had fallen from near the peak of a tobacco barn earlier that year, breaking his neck. When Mom tells the story today, her voice falters as she remembers how close she came to losing him. The break was high. He was not paralyzed; he recovered completely, and she has been forever grateful.

◆　◆　◆

I was their first child, born on November 4, 1952, the day Dwight Eisenhower became president of the United States. As the story goes, Mom began to feel labor pains about two o'clock in the morning. They went anxiously to the hospital, and all went as planned until after the birth.

"My womb did not close. I nearly bled to death," she tells me. "Dad was in the waiting room. You know in those days the fathers weren't allowed in the birthing rooms. He saw Dr. Prowell racing by but didn't realize what was happening until it was over. It was a freak thing. And it never happened with any of my children after that."

When she was strong enough to bring me home, my mother and father began a lifetime of nurturing me (and the ten other children who followed) in the ways of Amish faith, culture, and community.

◆　　◆　　◆

It was the 1950s and 1960s. People sometimes wondered whether the structures of modern life were indeed coming apart. We Amish were not untouched by the turmoil of American life.

As had been the case from the time our ancestors came to North America, we attended public schools. But we were not ready for the changes created by the consolidation movement of the 1950s.

One-room public schools within walking distance of our farms and homes were one thing. Huge yellow buses, whose destinations were architecturally imposing and uninviting structures, where we were lost in the crowd and where our parents felt unwelcome and unsure, were something else again.

How could our parents feel safe sending us to a place they did not understand?

How could they learn to trust a system designed to change the values they were trying to teach?

How did mandatory participation in instrumental music classes or the requirement that we wear uniforms to gym classes enhance their desire to raise us in the Amish faith?

Many Amish came to believe such ideas and activities threatened to destroy a carefully maintained community fabric. Parents simply could not, in good conscience, send their children out into this "world." So some refused. Several Amish fathers found themselves in jail.

That prospect brought on a debate between my parents late one summer Sunday evening. Our horse and buggy moved slowly along the rural Bachmantown Road while they tried to decide whether they should or should not send their children to school.

My father was determined he would not be so foolish as to disobey a law which would result in his being torn from his growing family.

They decided we would go to school, even if it meant getting on a school bus and riding to a distant location. We did. In retrospect, I think that must have been one of their first conscious steps away from the Old Order Amish church.

Some years later they would choose to leave the Old Order Amish church for a more progressive group called the Beachy Amish. While certain conveniences—automobiles, telephones, and electrical appliances—were accepted by this group, the basic tenets of Amish faith and life, even today, remain central to Beachy Amish understandings. The world is still a place to be separate from.

◆ ◆ ◆

These many years later I take a break from my computer screen and stare out my office window, looking out over the busy main street of Intercourse, Pennsylvania. I watch a middle-aged Amish woman walk smartly down the sidewalk. Her black shawl and bonnet provide a striking contrast to the mounds of white snow covering the ground this February day.

I wonder how much like my mom is this woman?

How many children does she have?

Does she like being Amish?

I think about my mother. She lives two miles from Intercourse, as the crow flies. I imagine her bent over her ever-present quilt frame, the current passion of her life. (She operates a small retail quilt shop.)

I know Mom likes being plain.

Now that she has a growing brood of grandchildren, by whom she is often royally entertained, I think she also likes having eleven children. She laughs with abandon at the antics of her grandsons and granddaughters, some of whom have quite un-Amish lives.

She also sometimes chides us for our ideas and conversations, occasionally stopping us dead in our tracks with the proclamation, "But the Bible says . . ." While it might be possible to argue with the Bible, we usually decide not to take on both Mother and the Bible.

◆ ◆ ◆

My mother is a fortunate woman. For she found a man to share her life whom she admired, trusted, and loved. Still together after forty-three years, they are beginning to enjoy the fruits of retirement.

They sometimes disagree. She is occasionally irritated by his lifelong habit of asking her for things, rather than getting them himself. He is occasionally distressed by her overreactions to life's problems.

Much more often, though, they sit together, trading ideas about some major life event, usually speaking in their native tongue—Pennsylvania Dutch.

They talk about the Los Angeles earthquake.

About granddaughter Sharla's tonsils.

About a position their church has taken.

Or about daughter Esther's soon-to-arrive baby.

◆　◆　◆

Everything my mother is and does and says is informed by her Amishness. Usually her world is a comforting microcosm. It is so when she moves from day to day through her regular activities— cooking, cleaning, sewing, quilting, visiting. She spends hours talking to her sisters, most of whom have always lived within only a few miles of her home.

They visit about each other's children.

Each other's churches.

Each other's hobbies.

Each other's deepest personal longings.

They also occasionally get together to do something special for one of their many children or grandchildren.

Such an event brought my mother and her sisters together several years ago.

♦ ♦ ♦

When I was eight years old, Grandmother Mary gave me a collection of beautifully cross-stitched quilt patches. She labored for hours over the creation of the forty-eight patches, each of which featured one state bird and state flower. (Alaska and Hawaii were not yet states.)

My mother put the exquisite pieces into her chest for safekeeping, waiting for the appropriate time to piece them into a quilt. I never married, and another logical time never seemed to come.

So I was pleasantly surprised when she brought up the subject again. "You know, Louise, I would really like to finish that quilt for your fortieth birthday." I eagerly agreed, and we set out to bring a piece of Grandmother Mary's work to life. We invited all of the aunts to a two-day quilting, asking them to invite their own daughters and granddaughters as well.

Many arrived early with their quilting needles, thimbles, scissors, and covered dishes of food. Expert fingers guided threaded needles across the quilt as conversation flowed above it. Occasional jokes about people who quilt too slowly or too quickly prompted easy laughter. Stories of husbands and brothers and sons were interspersed with peals of mirth over someone's forgetfulness; "We're all getting older you know."

References to Grandmother Mary filled the day. "Did you know purple was her favorite color? She would really like this quilt." Questions about family problems sometimes halted the quilting as everyone stopped to look up and hear the story from an aunt or cousin or granddaughter. The easy camaraderie sometimes veiled the pain, but it also opened doors for healing. Talking seemed to help make the problems less imposing, less frightful.

When the two days were finished and the last stitches came together at the quilt's center, I took home a work of art, completed with four generations of needlework and love.

◆　◆　◆

On another morning several summers ago, Mom walked out to open her quilt shop, a small unattached shed about one hundred feet from the house. She unlocked the door, realizing immediately that something had happened. Things were in disarray and quilts were missing.

Momentarily dazed, she walked around to the back of the shed. Someone had broken and crawled through the tiny back window. In his or her haste to flee, several quilts had been dropped on the lawn leading to the road. My mother anxiously recovered those precious pieces, not yet believing her eyes. As was customary in those days, she was home alone. Slowly taking stock of her situation, she began to understand.

Someone had broken into her shop.

Someone had stolen some of her quilts.

A call to the local police brought them out, but no one was ever apprehended. Absorbing the loss was perhaps the easiest part of that time in my mother's life. She also spent hours telling her story to each of her children and to her many friends. Over and over again, she said, "I just felt so unsafe."

◆　　◆　　◆

It is at such times that the world overwhelms women like my mother. It is a scary place. It is, after all, not safe, this world from which they separate themselves.

Most of the time my mother cannot fathom why I am not equally frightened of it.

Sometimes, though, she surprises me.

Like the time about a year ago when I told her about an upcoming business trip to New Orleans. Out of the blue she said, "New Orleans. That's a place I've always wanted to visit. I would really like to see the old plantation homes and the beautiful iron work."

Just for her I spent a day driving up the Mississippi from New

Orleans, stopping at some of the restored antebellum homes and bringing back pictures and stories.

The French Quarter, however, she would not have enjoyed, which she acknowledged, admonishing me to be careful. I was careful.

◆　◆　◆

These are the women who nurtured me.

My grandmothers.

My mother.

My mother's sisters.

My father's sisters.

They taught me how to cook, how to clean, how to sew, and how to quilt. They also taught me about limits. Some of which I have chosen not to heed. But all of which I respect and understand. All of which I know to be the ways of Amish women.

CHAPTER FOUR

She Likes Being Amish

For me it is, quite literally, a drive down memory lane. The one-lane gravel path which I remember has been replaced by a smartly paved rural road. The farmstead, though, looks much as it always has. Even the old smokehouse, now missing its roof, still stands on the high bank above the house. During my childhood I had often come to this place—the home of one of my father's sisters and her family.

As I drive into the farm lane, my cousin John, who now owns his father's farm, carries the youngest of his six children along the walkway from the barn toward the house. It is the same path where his younger brothers and I had often laughed and played, whiling away many hours of an Amish Sunday afternoon. When I meet him at the door, John opens his home with the same sincerity and warmth which I remember in his mother.

◆ ◆ ◆

I have come to visit with the woman who became John's wife. A woman whom I have admired and respected since the day we met. Susie and I sit by her kitchen table, sipping coffee and talking about the meaning of life while John returns to his woodshop in the barn.

She has chosen a path quite different from the way chosen by most Amish women. She is a watercolor artist. In addition to her busy life as a wife and mother, she tries to find at least ten to fifteen hours a week for painting. Her studio is her kitchen table, and several of her original watercolor paintings line the walls of her house.

"I have always been creative. I remember coloring until I had calluses on my fingers when I was a child. In school I loved when the teacher asked us to do freehand drawings."

From sixth to eighth grades, Susie's teacher was Anna Hurst. Also an artist, Anna taught Susie how to blend colors, how to do shadows, and how to work with tempera.

"She awakened my spirit."

Then at the end of Susie's last year in school, Anna gave her an elaborate watercolor paint set. Susie's eyes glow and she gestures warmly, "I remember thinking she *knew* exactly what I wanted."

◆ ◆ ◆

As a teenager, Susie drew and painted in her spare time. It seemed, though, that her sensibilities as an Amish young person provided little room for the idea that she might be an artist. Painting became a secondary interest, but the passion never left.

In the early years of their marriage, she and John were caught up in their new life together. They were young and trying to make a living on his father's farm. They worked hard and long hours. Susie helped in the fields. They got up every morning before the sun to milk their large herd of holsteins. There was precious little extra time.

"Today I sometimes wonder why I didn't paint during those years, rather than waiting until we had the children."

John and Susie were married nine years before they had children.

She notes reflectively that perhaps she needed the children to give her the sense of personal fulfillment required to sustain her life as an artist.

◆ ◆ ◆

Before her marriage, and again before their children came, Susie also occasionally taught school. It was the 1970s. Amish families had won the right to educate their own children. The 1972 U.S. Supreme Court decision—Wisconsin v. Yoder—decreed that

Amish children could no longer be forced to attend large consolidated school systems.

The Amish rose to the occasion. By the middle of the decade, there were seventy-some, one-room Amish schools operating in Lancaster County, Pennsylvania. They were built, funded, and run by the local, geographical church districts. Those responsible for the day-to-day operation of school life usually lived within two or three miles of the small building which their children attended.

Most parents were interested in making sure the schools provided a good, solid elementary education. In the years since the high court's decision, these tiny institutions have become an integral part of the Amish landscape and community.

◆　◆　◆

In 1974 I was hired to teach at the Meetinghouse Road Amish school, about two miles from John and Susie's farm. At my request, the school board also hired Susie to teach the required German classes. Once a week I picked her up during my afternoon recess and watched as she charmed the youngsters with the intricacies of their mother tongue.

One year as the time approached for the annual Christmas program, Susie and I decided to include something different from the usual fare of plays about gift-giving, poems which spelled out "Merry Christmas," and nativity pageants.

"Why not write a play about Amish life and have the children perform it in Pennsylvania Dutch?" Susie asked. She soon had one written. The children loved the idea, and we set about practicing.

In most Amish schools, Christmas has always been a festive time. The drudgery and boredom of daily learning are replaced with the excitement of preparing for "the program." Then as now, school districts varied in the amount of freedom they gave to the teacher. Meetinghouse Road was a relatively progressive school.

We always set out to do a show.

Fathers spent part of a Saturday constructing a stage. Mothers agreed to help with simple costumes for Mary and Joseph, wise men and shepherds. On the scheduled evening, the entire local Amish community streamed into the gaslit schoolroom, brimming with excitement and energy.

From the tiniest first-grader to the main character of the main play, all the students proudly prepared for the big moment when the homemade curtains would go up.

Susie's "Dietsch plays" became the highlight of those yearly events. People enjoyed watching elements of their own lives played out by their children.

In fact, these twenty years later, Susie's plays are still making the rounds in Amish schools, she tells me.

◆ ◆ ◆

Cousin John has returned from the barn and joins our conversation. As he settles into a rocking chair beside the stove, the topic shifts to the day of their wedding.

Twenty-five years earlier, he had invited me to be one of the attendants at his wedding. I was a starstruck sixteen-year-old. While I was quite unsure about the path of my own life, I was still Amish and I was deeply honored.

Amish weddings are usually private matters until about two weeks before they actually happen. While rumors always fly with decided abandon as the wedding season approaches (in Lancaster County most couples marry during November and early December), people seldom make official statements about dating or engagements or marriage. Instead, the community relies on unusual and even amusing indications that a wedding may be in the works.

The time-honored telltale sign of an eastern Pennsylvania Amish wedding is found in, of all places, the family garden.

Celery is indispensable to a traditional Amish wedding meal. It is the most important seasoning in the stuffing which is served with either chicken, duck, or turkey. It is sliced and served as a condiment. And the meal would not be complete without the exquisite cooked and creamed celery served as the main vegetable dish.

When a daughter plans to marry, she tells her parents early enough in the spring so they can put out a large patch of celery. Thus, how much celery a family plants is often cited as proof that there will or will not be a wedding.

Only with their closest friends and relatives will the couple actually confirm their plans. Cousin John's girlfriend, Susie, lived in Lebanon County, and my parents were not acquainted with her family.

We had not seen their celery patch!

◆　◆　◆

So I was surprised to be invited to join the wedding party about a month before the event. Mom quickly made a dress from material Susie sent to me. I learned that I would be spending the day with one of Susie's brothers. One other couple would also attend them.

November 12, 1968. We awoke to six inches of new snow on the ground. The van driver, hired by my father to take us to the wedding, arrived very early in the morning. We picked up an uncle and aunt and my grandparents and began the thirty-five-mile trip to Susie's home on the treacherous, snow-covered roads. We were late, and the wedding party was nervously awaiting my arrival.

With my mother close behind, I was hurried to a second-floor bedroom where the finishing touches were put on my royal blue dress, white cape, apron, and head covering. All the pins were quickly checked, and I was declared ready for the slow march down the curving stairway into the first floor. There we gathered on a long bench and quickly shook hands with all the invited guests before being ushered to our seats of honor near the long row of somber looking bishops and preachers.

It was an eventful and memorable day. The long morning church service and marriage ceremony were followed by an afternoon and evening of feasting, singing, and revelry.

I was shepherded from place to place as the wedding party made its various official appearances at the heavily laden tables, in the rooms where the gifts had been gathered, and in the cold storage area where all the beautifully decorated cakes and desserts were displayed for everyone to see.

I was only sixteen. This was the stuff of fantasy.

◆　◆　◆

John remembers that our grandfather had suffered a stroke several months before the wedding, making it impossible for him to preach the wedding sermon as John had wished. John also remembers Dawdy, as we called him, assuring him he would not miss the wedding. He didn't. "He was kind of tottery that day."

Susie says, "Our wedding was like almost all other Amish weddings. One main difference between how things were done when we got married and how they are done now had to do with the young people going to the table. In our day the boys still always asked the girls."

"Going to the table" during Amish wedding season is the highlight of many a young man's or woman's life. Two couples (usually married siblings of the bride and groom or other close relatives) are appointed to make sure everything goes according to the traditions and usual customs. Called fore-goers, they are also responsible for orchestrating an enchanting afternoon and evening ritual.

After everyone has been served the sumptuous noon meal, the two women fore-goers invite all the unmarried women between the ages of sixteen and about thirty to gather in one of the large upstairs bedrooms. The two men head for the stripping room, a room in the barn which is used during the winter months for the preparation and packaging of the farm's tobacco crop. Because the area is usually heated, the unmarried men often stand around the stripping room, joking and visiting on wedding days.

It is the fore-goers' task to convince as many of the young men as possible to go with them to the house. Once inside the house, the fore-goers lead them upstairs to a room where the girls are waiting. One by one, the men step up to the door of the room and choose a woman to "go to the table." They join hands and slowly descend the stairway into the first floor where they sit around the same long tables which were used to serve the noon meal.

The older folks assemble on benches throughout the house, and everyone joins in a rousing time of hymn-singing. While all the lyrics are German, familiar tunes like those for "What a Friend We

Have in Jesus" and "Neither Do I Condemn Thee" echo from the walls.

Bowls of festively decorated treats—candies, fruits, cakes, and cookies—are passed for everyone's pleasure. Those couples who enjoy singing and each others' company often sit for several hours. As twilight begins to fall, the bride and groom with their attendants leave the table, signaling the end of the afternoon activity and the beginning of evening preparations.

What happens next is the fascinating second chapter of the "going to the table" ritual. The women, especially those who enjoy flirting or who are brave, also find their way, always in groups of friends, to the stripping room. There, in the charged atmosphere of coupling, much like a dance, the young people mill about, talking and laughing.

The bride and groom are the center of the action because it is their task to make sure every unmarried young person has a partner for the evening table. Unlike the afternoon, participation is not optional. Those who are not interested either go home or find their way to a small table hidden away in the kitchen where they are served.

Susie explains, "When we got married, the boys still always asked the girls. Nowadays, the bride has to do all the pairing herself. If a boy wants a certain girl, he has to tell the bride."

By early evening the bride and groom have finished all the arrangements, often making quick last-minute adjustments for those who aren't happy. Meanwhile, the married folks have been served the evening meal, the gas lanterns have been lit, and the house has taken on a romantic warmth, aglow with expectation.

The girls are first to make their way from the stripping room to the house. They gather in animated groups in the various bedrooms on the second floor, excitedly comparing notes, combing hair, and adjusting dresses, capes, aprons, and coverings.

Not a moment too soon the boys are spotted making their way up the steps, with the fore-goers again leading the way. The bride and groom step from one of the rooms and, with their attendants, lead the procession. Following a seating arrangement set up by the bride and her fore-goers, the young people line up and slowly move down the stairs into the bustling first floor, each couple holding hands.

It is now late evening, and after a satisfying meal and lots of good conversation, the hymnbooks are passed around again, and everyone joins in the festivities. Those who are having a good time are often loath to leave, and many of the young couples will stay at the table as late as ten or eleven o'clock.

◆　◆　◆

Our conversation turns to John and Susie's children. "I think we have a nice family," Susie says, referring to their three sons and three daughters. While we visit, John cradles their preschooler on his lap and soothes him to sleep with a Pennsylvania Dutch lullaby.

Their oldest son recently found steady employment as frame shop manager in the gallery that displays and sells Susie's paintings. They talk of his decisions, acknowledging that they aren't very Amish. After telling me about a high school home schooling curriculum, Susie says, "I encouraged him to go on to high school. I'm glad he's finally decided to work at it. Now he says he might want to go to college. I don't know about that."

Their spirit of caring for a child whose decisions do not mirror their own warms me anew as I sit in their sprawling farm kitchen.

The next four children are quite close in age. They are in school. Susie talks about how nice it is for them to have each other. They all like to do the same kinds of things, from sledding to playing games to working together. For Christmas, they each received a pair of roller blades, and they are anxiously awaiting spring when they can spend more time learning to use them.

As she speaks about her hopes for each child, Susie again becomes thoughtful, "I am happy with what each of my children is right now. Why wait until they are grown to see what they will become? Each one of my children is a whole and complete person right now. Too many of us think if we just have one more thing, we will be happy. This I try to instill in my children—to be content with what they have. To be themselves right now.

"This is also how I feel about myself, even as an artist. The point is not to become great; the point is to keep learning and growing—yes—but also to be who I am now. And to be content."

◆　◆　◆

That is the great passion of Susie's life. To be content with who she is as an artist. While the Amish church has never said she should not paint, Susie has had intense personal struggles, juggling her gifts with her responsibilities.

Her family.

Her husband.

Her home.

Her community.

She is determined that painting will not become an obsession. After having developed a relationship with a local gallery a number of years ago and experiencing success as well as financial reward, Susie felt herself becoming too consumed.

◆　◆　◆

How well I remember an extended family reunion where Susie and I talked about that struggle. It was about a year after the birth of their youngest son, and John and Susie had invited all the cousins, aunts, and uncles for an evening get-together on their farm. After several hours of the usual back-and-forth banter of large family gatherings, many of us found ourselves in the kitchen helping to put away food. As we finished, I stood next to Susie and asked her how her life had been lately.

With the little fellow perched on her hip, she spoke briefly of her dilemma, cradling him into her shoulder as she said, "I'm coming to understand that he and my other children are much more important than painting."

Several months later she stopped painting. "It was like a death. I did not paint for six months. Until I finally came to terms with myself and came to understand that God doesn't mind if I do this."

A woman who loves to talk about ideas, she turns philosophical about her place in history. "I read once that a Christian can be an artist, but never a great artist. Take van Gogh, for example. He just went away from his life. He forgot about everything and everyone and just painted. I can't do that." She is wistful, but she knows that she has chosen well.

◆ ◆ ◆

I tell Susie that I think she would be exactly the same person even if she were not Amish. For a moment, she agrees. Then she shakes her head vigorously, "No."

With deep conviction, she explains herself, "As you know, we Amish are not perfect. All the elements of life which are morally wrong are present in our society. We are not free of any human problem."

Then Susie's voice changes and she looks full into my eyes. It is her abiding personal faith in the central truths of Amish understandings which holds her life together. It is her strong belief in the centrality of community and family which provides safety and satisfaction. It is her hope in the Amish way which makes her world complete.

A woman of deep intuition and striking intelligence, Susie turns to me as I prepare to leave.

"I like being Amish," she says.

CHAPTER FIVE

Of Doughnuts and Children

Naomi is one of those women who finds life as a homemaker, as a caregiver to children, completely satisfying. She has a slim, beautiful face with wispy chestnut hair which is neatly combed and tucked beneath her head covering. She welcomes me into her sunny, spacious home on an icy winter morning. Almost immediately, it feels familiar and warm.

The piquant smell of yeast and dough permeates the air.

The bustle of an Amish kitchen suddenly surrounds me.

The children are all home from school.

Mother Naomi is presiding over a once-a-year doughnut-making project. Everyone is encouraged to join in, but it is the four middle children who are most involved. Kathryn, Raymond, Anne, and James. I watch as twelve-year-old Kathryn kneads the dough, while Mom gives helpful pointers in Pennsylvania Dutch. Naomi keeps a close watch on the fryer where the oil comes slowly to the perfect temperature. Fingers and hands start busily shaping the dough.

She slips easily from English to Dutch, always addressing comments to her children in her native tongue. I understand, but she senses it is difficult for me to speak this language of my family and home. So when she turns to me, she moves smoothly back to English.

Nobody stops working. Talk and task ebb and flow around the kitchen. Everyone listens with interest and wonder. No doubt questions will fill the air in Naomi's kitchen after I leave, as her children try to understand their mother's connection to me.

She reminds me of something I have long since forgotten.

We were in our mid-twenties. We were both teaching in one-room Amish schools. She at Pinecrest. I at Meetinghouse Road. She says she remembers me from the "teacher classes"—periodic and well planned times when Amish teachers gather at one of the area's many schools to trade ideas and learn from each other.

At first I cannot remember. Then it slowly dawns on me. We knew each other when I was still Amish but have not seen each other in twenty years.

"Oh my," I say, "Now I remember."

I remember that she was one of Susie's friends.

I remember that occasionally she traveled with me to one or another of the teachers' get-togethers.

The divergent paths of our lives come together for me with a sense of wonder and surprise. Could this dynamic mother woman, immersed in the care of her family, be the same person I had known? I see the same question mirrored in her eyes. Could this woman of the world possibly be the same person she had known? I feel that she is, indeed, the same person. Perhaps a bit weathered and changed by the years. What she thinks of me is unspoken in her gentle, but direct manner.

◆　◆　◆

The doughnuts have reached the deep-frying stage. They have no holes, for they will soon be filled with a smooth, rich frosting made with confectioners' sugar, shortening, egg whites, flour, vanilla, and milk. Mouths start to water.

Everybody takes a break, and I am invited to join in, enjoying the first rich fruits of their labor. The delicate deep-fried dough and its filling melt on the tongue. It is a rare winter morning treat.

◆ ◆ ◆

Naomi supervises as the children turn to cleaning up the project. She tells me, "I taught school for eight years. Elmer and I did not marry until I was twenty-seven."

I ask her how they met.

"At the teachers' classes." Again, it comes to me slowly. One of only two or three Amish men who taught school during our time, Elmer is someone I remember from those meetings. It does not surprise me that they connected.

Both are deeply committed to the Amish way.

Both are intelligent and sensitive.

Both are willing to share their faith.

Both are cautious of exploitation and misunderstanding.

Today they operate a twenty-acre produce farm next door to the picturesque farmstead where Elmer grew up. On this early March day, he is deeply engrossed in his other occupation. He works as an accountant and is preparing income taxes in his office. I do not see Elmer until late morning when he takes a brief break and comes to the house looking for some of those delicious doughnuts.

As he returns to his office, the children produce a Carom board, and several of them join in the fun. Naomi begins preparing the noon meal, and we decide to continue our conversation some other time.

◆ ◆ ◆

When I visit Naomi again, her middle children are all in school. She offers me tea with honey and joins me at the kitchen table, reaching for the two youngest ones as they move into her lap. Her small daughter asks for tea in Pennsylvania Dutch. She is immediately accommodated.

Again I wonder at the way Naomi has with her children. It seems to me a particular gift. I think about where it comes from.

Her upbringing.

Her enduring personal faith.

Her union with an equal partner.

Her devotion to home and family.

Silently I celebrate for the seven young souls growing up in this place, with this mother and this father.

◆　◆　◆

Our conversation turns to the births of their children. "When I was carrying our oldest son, we believed having him in a hospital would provide the best of care. I read everything I could find on childbirth. We went to Lamaze classes, and I felt prepared for the birth.

"Everything at the hospital was different than I expected. It was horrible. The delivery was long and difficult.

"When my baby finally came, I just wanted to hold him. But, of course, they took him away so I could rest and recover. I wanted my baby.

"I had not eaten for twenty-four hours, and I was so hungry. It was midnight, so, of course, they didn't offer me food. I felt I would disturb the nurses if I asked for something to eat, so I suffered in silence. It seemed to me that at the hospital everything normal about childbirth was inconvenient."

Not having children of my own, I ask Naomi lots of questions. After their first child, she tells me, she and Elmer began exploring the idea of employing a midwife.

It was the early 1980s, and the practice of midwifery was regarded with some suspicion. Emerging from an era concerned primarily with "progress," many North Americans had come to believe that modernity demanded new ways of doing most everything in life, including giving birth.

Justifiably concerned about infant mortality rates, many healthcare providers convinced parents that sterile hospital rooms were safer places to have children. During the worst years of this trend, fathers suffered through the pain of being banned from delivery rooms. They sat in antiseptic waiting rooms while their companions were supervised and guided by highly trained professionals. Some of these professionals suggested formula was better for children than mother's milk, convincing many women to forego nursing their babies. Throughout this time, many Amish women clung to a desire to have their children in familiar safe surroundings. At home.

In Lancaster County, most of them called on Dr. Grace Kaiser. A woman doctor who began her practice in the Amish community in 1950, she confounded everyone with her straightforward, unapologetic desire to make sure those Amish women who wanted to could continue to give birth at home.

I remember hearing one of my mother's sisters talk about *Dochtah Frau* (Doctor Woman), as Kaiser was affectionately called among the Amish. All of Aunt Barbara's children came into the world in the bedroom of her humble farm home with Dr. Kaiser's help.

Grace Kaiser refused to be swung by modern opinion. Throughout the twenty-eight years of her practice, she made sure Amish women, such as my mother's sister, were treated with dignity and respect. When her practice came to an abrupt end following an accident in 1978, the Amish community found itself facing a new dilemma.

Young women such as Naomi and her friends believed hospitals, doctors, and Lamaze classes were probably good solutions to their problem. But many found themselves longing for *Dochtah Frau*.

◆　◆　◆

This longing was satisfied with the coming of certified nurse midwives. In the late 1980s, several midwives set up offices in Lancaster County, finding the Amish quite receptive to their services.

In many places, midwives are still pioneers within the medical community. They are usually strong characters, willing to face down the ideas about childbirth promoted during "the age of progress." They put up with impossible hours, answering their phones and going out to remote farms and homes any hour of the night or day. They make a difference for many, many Amish women, and their zeal has been an incomparable gift to people like Elmer and Naomi. Naomi says that today most of her friends employ midwives to assist them in childbirth.

◆　◆　◆

Rather than rushing to a hospital in a stranger's car, Naomi now sends Elmer to call the midwife when her contractions begin. She puts a kettle of soup on the stove and stays up, moving around the kitchen to keep herself comfortable. "Elmer is always with me, and we often play Scrabble here at the kitchen table.

"I love having my children at home.

"It is so convenient.

"So natural.

"So normal."

◆　◆　◆

Elmer and Naomi are avid readers. They are members of several book clubs. They subscribe to *Family Life*, *Young Companion*, and *Blackboard Bulletin*, periodicals distributed by Pathway Publishers, an Amish owned and operated publishing house. They also enjoy farming publications such as *Farm and Ranch Living* and *Country Woman*.

Naomi's favorite writer, however, is C.S. Lewis. From the Narnia series to a recent novel based on Lewis's life, she believes she has read almost everything written by or about the mid-twentieth century English children's author, novelist, and essayist.

I have recently seen *Shadowlands*, the moving film story about C.S. Lewis and Joy Gresham, the American woman who became his wife. Naomi has just finished reading *Shadowlands*, the novel by Leonore Fleischer on which the movie's screenplay is based.

To me, C.S. Lewis will forever look like Anthony Hopkins. And Joy Gresham will always be Debra Winger. I wonder how Naomi pictures them. We compare notes, agreeing our images of Lewis and Gresham are different, but that the love story is, indeed, one for the ages.

CHAPTER SIX

Of Swiss Chalets and Amish Roots

Linda is the oldest child and only daughter in a family known among the Amish for its adventuresome spirit and straightforward style. Unlike some of her brothers, Linda, who is sixty-eight years old and single, preferred to stay close to home. She gave much of her life to caring for her aging parents.

Soon after World War II, one brother spent several years in Germany with PAX, a Mennonite-based relief program. He met and married a German woman who moved to the United States with him. They chose not to join the Amish church, but his new wife, Lydia, brought with her a strong sense of European manners and grace, which intrigued her Amish in-laws. It was Lydia's influence, Linda says, which led their Amish father to build a Swiss chalet-style house for his retirement home.

That home has long been a fixture in the neighborhood. I have seen it many times, but I am still charmed.

By its lines.

By its character.

By its window boxes overflowing with flowers.

◆　◆　◆

As an Amish teenager, I had been best friends with several of Linda's nieces—the daughters of another one of her brothers. We were young. We liked being Amish. We had lots of good times together—singing and talking and laughing. We occasionally spent Sunday afternoons at the Swiss chalet, singing for their grandparents and their beloved Aunt Lin, as they called her.

We grew up.

Got older.

Lost touch with each other.

And each other's roots.

◆　◆　◆

These many years later, I park my car at the top of the steep bank which leads to the house. Linda meets me at the door with Emma, her eight-month-old great-niece, cooing and smiling contentedly in her arms. Loaves of bread "just out of the oven" line the kitchen counter and fill the air with their distinctive aroma.

With apologies that she needs to give Emma her breakfast, Linda invites me to pull up the pillowed rocker and puts Emma into a sturdy, old-fashioned wooden high chair, which looks to have held several generations of this family's children.

In the typical way of the Amish, we take the first few minutes to make connections. I know her nieces and nephews. She knows my parents and aunts and uncles. We each remember the other from different times and places.

She wears distinguished wire-rim glasses and has a strong, almost wiry, constitution. The half-inch wide strings of her muslin head covering are draped casually over her shoulders. She appears much younger than she is.

A member of the same Amish church district her entire life, Linda was born and raised less than a mile from where she now lives. She went through all eight grades of her school-going years at the one-room school which still stands within sight of what once was her mother's kitchen window. Much of her life has revolved around this tiny crossroad village and its close-knit Amish neighborhood. These deep roots, however, have not kept her from occasionally trying her wings.

Every Saturday evening, she tells me, her father would make a trek to the Mabel Myers village store in another nearby town to catch up on the latest local gossip and world events. She and her three brothers usually went with him, looking forward to the promised piece of candy. Listening in on the talk around the old woodstove, Linda first came to feel what it might be like to leave her neighborhood.

"I love horses. I started driving a carriage at age fourteen. And I've had a horse and buggy ever since. As a young person, I would drive any horse Dad let me, whether or not it was completely broken."

In 1973 Linda and one of her friends embarked on what for two Amish women was the excursion of a lifetime. A trip to Europe. Because the Amish church requests that its members not use airplanes for travel, Linda and her friend decided to take an ocean liner. The *Queen Elizabeth II*.

They spent four weeks traveling around France, Switzerland, and Germany with Eurrail passes and a spirit for adventure. Linda tells me that speaking Pennsylvania Dutch, which is a German dialect, made communication relatively easy. "I especially enjoyed Passau."

◆　◆　◆

While Linda does have an adventurous streak, I am most interested in her decided refusal to dwell on what her life might be like if she were not Amish. Like most Amish women, she lives in the present, not in the past or even the future.

It is better, it seems to Linda, to be content with life as it is.

That is not to say she has no personal preferences or that she never thinks or talks about other ways of being and doing. She does. She just doesn't dwell on them.

In that resolve, I find particular strength. It creates a place of peace, a place of rest, a place to be, and to stay, Amish.

◆　◆　◆

To Linda, personal privacy is an important consideration. She knows that who she is and how she lives is an increasing curiosity. Visitors stream into Lancaster County to learn about the Amish. Many do not believe what they see, sometimes thinking they have stumbled into still another version of Colonial Williamsburg. So they ask questions, sometimes thinking they are interrupting a costumed interpreter, not a real-life person with work to do and places to go. Many visitors know better but still cannot help themselves.

Who are you?

How do you live?

What can you tell us about yourself?

Because Linda likes to talk to people and enjoys making new friends, she often opens herself to the questioners. And finds it frustrating. For even a bit of openness means she may be inundated with requests. Requests that she finds difficult to deny, but which interfere with the treasured daily routine of her life. It is a privacy only she can protect.

◆　◆　◆

As she talks about her dilemma, I remember an event from my childhood. I was six years old and we lived along a back country road. My mother had tied the horse and buggy to the fence. She told my four brothers and me to wait outside while she went back to the house for the baby.

While we waited, a car stopped along the nearby road, and a man carrying a camera came toward us. I hurriedly got into the buggy. The photographer asked my brothers if they would stand beside the buggy and persuaded me to open the buggy door so he could see me. Mom, who preferred not to have her own picture taken, watched apprehensively from the house. After clicking his camera numerous times, he gave each of us a dime and left, smiling his thanks.

Yes, our privacy had been invaded.

Yes, we were delighted with the dimes.

Yes, such experiences are typical.

Yes, they are unavoidable.

As Amish, we lived in the world. Our parents were choosing, therefore, to interact with the world. They did not wish to escape the world. But they did wish to live separate lives. They knew they were "in the world," but they wished not to be "of the world."

To accomplish this feat—"in the world, but not of the world"—the Amish church has established guidelines. Nevertheless, its members are free to make some of their own decisions regarding how much or how little they will interact with the larger world. Some Amish women and men are very open to seekers and questioners. Others, without apology, always say no.

◆　◆　◆

I think about the way Linda lives without most of the world's conveniences, attitudes, or practices. Yet within the definitions of her gathered community, she still exercises an amazing amount of freedom.

Linda shops at local grocery stores, rides public transportation, visits local doctors, dentists, and opticians, and interacts with people of the world.

She, like most Amish people, makes frequent adjustments to accommodate the changes in the world around her. But she refuses to get caught up in the world's philosophies—the hope of progress—or in, what seems to her, the misguided belief that new creations and inventions always provide better opportunities.

This way of living pervades Amish society and provides the foundation for the particular form of community life practiced by the Amish.

They do not live in enclosed communes. Each family unit has its own individual home. These homes are interspersed among the larger population. They live on rural farms. In small villages. In suburbs. And on the edges of medium-sized cities.

Linda is responsible and accountable to the community, but she is not bound by it. Within the definitions of Amish community life, she makes her own decisions and choices.

She cannot jet to Europe because airplanes are a modern convenience Amish society frowns upon. But she can take a leisurely ocean liner to see the world and stay in the good graces of her church.

She cannot own a car because the Amish have come to believe that automobiles provide too much freedom and too much opportunity to disappear from important family times together. They are too convenient. But Linda can have her own horse and buggy and come and go at will without answering to anyone. Or she can use public transportation.

She can and does live "in the world." The church, however, requires that she not be "of the world."

◆   ◆   ◆

Linda's life is integrated into the strong fabric of this unusual form of community life. Having lived with her parents her entire life, she quite naturally moved into the primary caretaker role when they became ill. Many Amish single women spend a large portion of their lives in such a role.

It is not always easy.

But it is almost always accepted with grace.

Amish children seldom consider admitting their aging parents to a nursing home. The place to grow old is at home, where all the other of life's important milestones happen.

Birth.

Baptism.

Marriage.

Daily work and play.

Retirement.

Death.

After Linda's mother died in 1976, she spent seven long years caring for her father through his agonizing battle with Alzheimer's. "I was so glad he could at least be at home in the house he had built with his own hands." Again, Linda does not dwell on what might have been. Rather, she believes, "This was what God wanted for me." She received her support from the community and from her many friends who had similar responsibilities.

◆ ◆ ◆

Through those years, she also kept her job as a cook at a local restaurant. She says, "I have lots of friends. And I think I have as much pleasure in my life as most people who are married."

She gets together with a group of Amish friends about once a month. Most are single women. They visit people who "can use some cheering up." Every year on Ascension Day they plan a major hiking excursion, enjoying the day out in "God's great creation." Occasionally they hire one of the many taxi services which cater to the Amish and travel to other nearby Amish communities for a day or a weekend.

"I wish there was better public transportation. I really liked the convenience of bus and rail service when we traveled in Europe." That wish, it seems to me, reflects the spirit of independence which I have always associated with her family.

The men are often interested in adventure.

The women are often fascinated by that.

And the children follow in their footsteps.

I watch as Linda turns to her great-niece, who has been squirming on her lap as we visit. Two days a week this bright-eyed and open-faced little girl comes to her Amish great-aunt's home while her parents work. She is loved and nurtured. She receives a strong, healthy dose of common sense, of determination, and of her roots. She is not Amish, but through Linda she is learning about those who came before her. Those people whose lives were deeply rooted in the Amish way. What a precious gift for a child of the twenty-first century.

CHAPTER SEVEN

Heaven Is of Great Interest

Soon after I arrive at Esther's home, she tells me a story. Esther, her husband David, and their family were attending the regularly scheduled biweekly Amish church service on a neighboring farm. On this particular Sunday morning, a minister from another Amish district was present and was asked to give the main morning sermon.

In the warm, lilting, singsong cadence of Amish preachers, he spoke about personal responsibility in the church. At one point, Esther says, he paused to ask the question, "Who has the most important role in the church? The deacon? The minister? The bishop?"

Turning to face the side of the room where most of the women were seated, he proclaimed, "No, it is not the deacon, the minister, or the bishop; it is the mothers with babies on their laps who have the most important task in our church." A hush fell over the already quiet room.

Mothers with babies on their laps snuggled them a bit closer.

Fathers nodded their heads ever so slightly.

Grandmothers dabbed at their eyes with handkerchiefs.

It was a special blessing to hear a church leader give colloquial voice, during what is usually a formal presentation, to this fundamental truth of Amish faith and understanding. The family is central. To be a mother is a high and holy calling.

Home is a place of life and hope.

A place to nurture and hold children.

A place to ensure posterity and success.

Perhaps it is the often quoted proverb from the writings of David, the psalmist, which best describes how most Amish feel about family life: "Lo, children are an heritage of the Lord: and the fruit of the womb is the Lord's reward. As arrows are in the hand of a mighty man; so are children of the youth. Happy is the one who has his quiver full of them."

◆ ◆ ◆

It is shattering, then, when a child dies. For Esther and David, such a tragedy struck early in their life together. Their first children—twin sons—were born in April of 1981. Seven months later, Sudden Infant Death Syndrome (SIDS) claimed one of the twins—little Johnny.

Esther says poignantly, "We were so young."

They had just rented and moved to a 100-acre farm at the northernmost end of the Lancaster Amish community. To cope, David and Esther channeled their energies and their grief into the toil of everyday life on the large farm, working out their sorrow in the soil which surrounded them. Over the next ten years, they had four other children.

They were happy.

The farm was thriving.

Their four sons and one daughter were healthy and content.

Esther devoted herself to helping with the farmwork, keeping house, and caring for the little ones—young David Jr. and his baby sister.

She notes that watching the children had become an important consideration. For a two-lane country road passes directly between the house and barn. When the buildings were put up in the late

1700s, it must have seemed a good choice to have the house and barn on opposite sides of what would have been little more than a path.

Two centuries later the decision seems much less wise. For the road, which is otherwise curvy and winding, happens to travel an open, straight path as it overtakes their home on a downward slope. Vehicles approach with decided abandon, oblivious that they are passing on a fragile barrier slicing through an Amish farm.

◆ ◆ ◆

So it was that in May of 1992 the Amish and the surrounding community were shocked and saddened to learn that one such fast-moving car had struck and killed David Jr. as he tried to cross between the barn and house.

As we sit by Esther's kitchen table on this Wednesday morning two years later, Esther turns to me and says, "Today it is exactly two years ago." Tears gather at the corners of her eyes, and I can only say, "I'm sorry." She tells me, "Yes, I thought about it when you asked if you could come today."

For a brief moment, I wish I had chosen a different day. However, she quickly goes on to say how important it has become to her to talk about their loss. I wonder if I can provide a listening ear for her on this day so full of pain and memory. For I find it difficult to talk about and am continually amazed by how easily she weaves her emotions into the stories she tells me.

"It was 6:30 in the evening. We were milking the cows. School had let out a couple days before. The boys had had a good year, and we had those few precious days as a complete family. Junior had been so looking forward to having his older brothers at home. We all always looked forward to that time of the year, for we loved having the whole family together." It was not to be. Instead, time stood still as the sound of screeching brakes surrounded the serene farmstead.

The family rushed to the scene.

Neighbors began gathering.

The police and an ambulance sped down the nearby rural roads.

The driver of the car stood by in shock.

"Right at the time I kept assuring him that we did not blame him." I marvel at such grace. What are its roots? From where does it come? I wonder.

I know it is from her faith. Indeed, grace and faith are completely integrated in this woman's life. For in the next sentence, she acknowledges that forgiving the driver has been much more difficult than she ever thought it would be. She has been deeply wounded; she has experienced enormous personal loss, but she is on a long journey of healing and wholeness which casts shadows over her face and suffuses her being. I feel tears gathering at the corners of my own eyes.

◆ ◆ ◆

Three months before young Junior's death, David and Esther had taken their family to be with their very good friends who had just lost a child. During the long afternoon and evening of the viewing, four-year-old Junior stood by the coffin as other people moved in and out of the room where the baby lay.

Esther says, "We did not know about this until after Junior's death. I just thought he was somewhere playing with the other children. After he died, the father came to us with this story. He told us that every time he took people into the room to pay their respects, Junior was always there. At one point, he picked him up and held him for a while, talking to him about death."

Esther remarks about how comforting it was to hear that story. She says, "We spent many hours just talking with these friends about our shared experiences."

Out of that time of sharing, Esther and David came to believe that they were called to reach out to others who suffered loss, especially the loss of a child.

69

Today they are known in the Amish community for the caring and understanding which they extend to people who are in mourning. In a conversation I had with one of Esther's friends, she said, "I love to watch David and Esther as they draw people out."

Esther concedes that it isn't easy. "But we do it gladly because we were always so grateful ourselves for those people who came and weren't afraid to talk about Junior. It was terribly hard when people came to visit and did not bring up the subject. We needed to talk about how we felt."

Esther's friend had told me a story. "Several months ago we went with David and Esther to visit Daniels"—a family whose grown bachelor son had been killed in a construction accident. The mother of the family was having an especially difficult time. "Esther was gentle and patient as she reached out to that deeply grieved woman. Before long, both parents were talking openly about their pain. I have learned so much about grief just by spending time with David and Esther."

I ask Esther whether she thinks of herself as a counselor. She says, "No, I think of myself as a friend. To me friendship, caring, and visiting are the gifts I can offer. David and I did not choose this. We would never have chosen this. But if we can help people, that is what we want to do."

◆　◆　◆

Esther comments that the Amish way of dealing with grief is unusual. Later she seems to completely reverse herself, noting that the experience of grief is the same for an Amish person as it is for any other person.

Having attended many Amish viewings and funerals myself, I understand why she makes that distinction. While the emotion and experience of grief are universal, it is true that the Amish community has its own way of dealing with grief.

For weeks and sometimes even months after a family experiences a loss, friends, family members, distant relatives, and acquaintances frequently drop by unannounced—usually in the evenings or on Sunday afternoons—to visit. Grieving persons expect people to come and are keenly disappointed if they receive few visitors.

The purpose is simply to show support; sometimes, as Esther sadly noted, people find it uncomfortable to articulate the obvious reason for their visit. "In the first weeks after the funeral, we would often have a whole houseful of company for most of Sunday afternoon and evening." She went on to say that it helped most to talk to people who had similar experiences and to hear people say they were sorry or that they missed Junior. "We Amish grieve just like all other people."

Indeed, grief is an encompassing emotion.

It reaches across time.

Across understandings.

Across cultures.

Esther and David have also been surprised by the ongoing support they receive from people who are not Amish in the community around the farm. Even the investigating police officer was moved by the incident. He has since become a close friend and visits them frequently.

When Esther and David began probing his unusual interest in them, they learned that he had a five-year-old son who filled his thoughts as he knelt beside Junior in the road. Because of a divorce, he had not seen the boy for several years. His encounter with tragedy on that deceptively quiet rural road prompted him to reconnect with his own son.

◆　◆　◆

Along with support from people around them, Esther and David also rely on a deep reservoir of personal faith. Like many Amish, they have an angel philosophy. Quoting from the Book of Revelation, the preacher in David and Esther's church district recently talked about the appearance and the dimensions of heaven. "Why does the Bible say that heaven is as high as it is wide and deep?

"I think that it must be to make room for the angels. The angels are not all on their feet. They are moving around the length and breadth and depth of heaven."

Esther looks at me with wistful eyes and says, "That gave me such a longing to see our angels again. I miss them so much."

It is Esther's profound belief in heaven and in angels which sustains her. "Dwelling on the beauty of heaven is the only way I can cope with the reality of losing Junior and Johnny. Death is the door to life." Her sons, she knows, live on.

They are angels.

She is comforted.

"Heaven is of great interest to me," she says.

◆　◆　◆

Losing Johnny to SIDS has actually helped David and Esther through the questioning and pain related to Junior's death. "The hardest thing we faced was wondering whether we had somehow not done our duty. Had we not been watching him closely enough? Were we to blame? Every time that comes up for any of us, we remember Johnny, and that finishes the questioning. For how can you keep a child from dying in its crib? We know that we could not possibly have prevented Junior's death either."

David and Esther have chosen to go on with their lives.

A riot of flowers—petunias, peonies, and marigolds—surrounds the house on this delightful spring morning. Rows of corn form an emerging pattern of green in the vast acreage around the farm's buildings. The garden glows with the obvious care and purpose of a family who will derive much sustenance from its yield.

While we are visiting, Esther sets up a quilt frame, displaying an exquisite Country Love wall hanging which she is making to sell. Her fingers move deftly, creating an intricate needlework pattern. She happens to have part of this day off from farm- and fieldwork because it is David's goal to finish planting the forty acres of corn.

The day before, Esther, David, and their three sons, ages eight, ten, and thirteen, worked most of the day bringing in the summer's first hay crop. The stinging sensation of freshly mown and baled hay still hovers over the farmstead. The large barn doors on the bank leading to the second floor stand wide open, taking advantage of the drying air.

Esther tells me she loves to help with farmwork because she can be together with her husband and her children. "We were unloading hay until almost dark. After the children were in bed, I looked in on them and thought about how good it was to be together."

While Esther helps a great deal with outside work, the lines between men's and women's work are, nevertheless, quite clear. David would not want her to harrow or disk or mow alfalfa. But she drives the horses for baling hay. She helps milk the cows. She plants, maintains, and harvests the garden. She watches and cares for their daughter. She keeps house and cooks the meals.

"For me, nothing is more satisfying than making meals," Esther remarks as she gets up to put a slab of homegrown beef into a kettle. As we sit talking, the meat cooks, flavoring the whole house with a mouthwatering aroma.

David enjoys having her outside.

Esther loves to be with him.

So they negotiate to accomplish the varied tasks of operating this 100-acre family farm. They are a team.

But they are also two separate people. She tries to remember that David does occasionally find it much more difficult to talk about the loss of their sons.

◆　◆　◆

Esther thinks they were too young to really know what was happening to them when Johnny died. When Junior died, many of the feelings about Johnny came back. So when the pain overwhelmed her, she started keeping a diary.

In the fall of 1993, she first showed the diary to some friends who urged her to think about transcribing it into a form which could be published. One of her non-Amish neighbors, who is a good friend, offered Esther the use of a computer. She hesitated.

After receiving much more encouragement, Esther finally decided to spend one day a week at her neighbor's house. She taught herself how to use the word processing system and transferred the diary into story form.

Gathering up all her courage, she sent it to a publishing house late in the winter of 1994. She received a promising letter and a phone call from an editor, indicating the publishing house had not decided for sure, but they were seriously considering her book.

I ask her whether she is ready to deal with the possible fame of being an Amish woman and an author. Will she be willing to make appearances and fill speaking engagements? "Well no," Esther says, "I probably could not do that.

"I wrote my book because I cannot stand the look of hopelessness and pain I see in people's eyes. I did not write it for fame or fortune. I wrote my story to touch those people, to give them hope, to take away some of their despair. Always, I just think I must help them."

CHAPTER EIGHT

I Love My Community

Decisive career person and devoted Amish woman. At first glance and even after extensive study, most people would conclude that nothing in Amish thought or practice allows for this combination.

But I find it embodied in a forty-year-old woman I first met when both of us were teaching in one-room Amish schools.

It was the mid-1970s. I had taken the day off from my own teaching responsibilities to visit other Amish schools and gather ideas. I knew Rebecca by reputation, having talked to her on occasion at one or another of our teachers' get-togethers. Because she was considered one of the best teachers in the Lancaster Amish community at that time, I decided to stop by her school. Struck by the abundance of fine, freehand paintings lining the walls of the one-room building, I asked her how it happened that she had so many artists as students.

"Well," she said, "I show them how, but they also have lots of

natural talent. It is there inside them. You just have to draw it out."
I remember being determined to impart something of equal value
to the youngsters in my charge.

Twenty years later, as we sit opposite each other in Rebecca's
kitchen on a late summer evening, I recount the event to jog her
memory. She thinks she might remember, but she cannot quite
make the connection. There is no reason why she should. I have
been gone for many years. Our lives are very different than they
were in the 1970s.

◆ ◆ ◆

I next saw Rebecca soon after I returned to Lancaster County in
the late 1980s. Looking to furnish a house, I often attended Amish
estate auctions, sometimes also finding artifacts which reminded
me of my life among the Amish.

At one such auction, I decided to bid on an old, rather
tattered-looking basket. It was like the basket my mother carried
on her arm to every church service I could remember as a child.
In it she usually kept fresh diapers and a change of clothes for the
baby, but she also always packed a small container of Cheerios
which I was permitted to eat halfway through the four-hour service.
Dry Cheerios still remind me of sitting close by my mother on long
Sunday mornings.

I paid twelve dollars for the basket. As the runner brought it back to me in the crowd, an Amish woman, standing directly in front of me, turned and said, "If you would like to get that fixed, there are some people who can make those baskets look like new." It was Rebecca. I thanked her, too embarrassed to tell her who I was or to tell her that I preferred for it to look old. No doubt she thought she had spoken to just another collector of Amish antiques.

As we sit together in her kitchen, I still do not tell her that story.

◆ ◆ ◆

Instead, I ask whether she thinks of herself as a career woman. Without a moment's hesitation, she says, "Yes."

These days Rebecca works long hours as a medical assistant to a non-Amish, Harvard-trained genetics researcher, Dr. Holmes Morton. They operate a clinic and high-tech care facility in the heart of the Amish community in Lancaster County's southern end.

She is single. When she leaves work behind and escapes to her oasis, she is surrounded by her family in an enclave of buildings which includes a large farmhouse where her brother and his wife live. A smaller attached house where her parents live in retirement. And across the lawn her own small house. That is where I find her.

She is pleasant and direct.

Passionate and deliberate.

Philosophical and matter-of-fact.

◆ ◆ ◆

Four years ago, after having spent fifteen years as an Amish school teacher, she decided to change course. The chance to work with Dr. Morton was too good to turn down.

Her voice rises several octaves as she hones in on the compelling ambition of her current life. "Our goal is to make high-tech medical care readily accessible to those people who need it most. Much of the equipment in our laboratory is found in only a few other places in the world. But there it stands in the middle of an Amish farmer's field."

The clinic has several part-time employees, but it is basically a two-person operation. Most of the patients are either local Amish or Mennonites, but its work is known throughout the medical community, and Rebecca says, "We have diagnosed patients from all over the United States."

They are on a quest to stabilize the effects of genetic disorders among the Amish. To bring hope to suffering parents. To bring healing to suffering children. "I happen to have five nieces and nephews who have glutaric aciduria, a debilitating genetic problem. All appeared completely normal and healthy at birth. Two have died. Of the three who are still living, one walks and talks and is only lightly afflicted. The other two are in wheelchairs."

It is easy to identify the source of Rebecca's passion. Like most Amish, she considers caring for childen and preserving the quality of their lives tantamount to godliness.

Though she has no children of her own, Rebecca is surrounded by little people. At work she pours all her energies into their care. Her one-year-old niece hovers around her feet as we talk, occasionally climbing into Rebecca's lap to be held and snuggled. The unmistakable sounds of little ones at play drift through the screen door from the lawn in front of her brother's house. She turns to me and says, "Being a homemaker is the most important job a woman can possibly have.

"But I also know that God chose for me to be single. I believe it is important to be useful in my sphere. What I care about is keeping children well."

◆ ◆ ◆

Keeping children well. Rebecca says the two main genetic disorders which the clinic addresses—maple syrup urine disease and glutaric aciduria—can be controlled if they are identified. For that reason, her job also includes education. Getting the word out to the Amish community that infants should be tested at birth has been one focus of her work. Getting the word out to the medical community which services the Lancaster County Amish has been another focus.

I ask her how those goals are accomplished.

She talks to Amish women. At church services. At family reunions. At weddings. At quiltings. At funerals. "Ask for the test when your child is born," she urges them.

If parents learn at birth that a newborn has glutaric aciduria, Rebecca says, the chances of keeping the child well increase dramatically. For it is the usual childhood diseases—measles, mumps, common colds, or ear infections—which cause the crippling brain damage of this particular disorder.

◆ ◆ ◆

Dr. Morton's clinic stands in the heart of the Amish community. It charges very little for its services. And it employs one of their own, a woman whom the Amish know and trust. For those reasons, Amish parents are much more likely to call the doctor when they suspect their child may need immediate medical attention.

"It is part of my job to coordinate care over the telephone. If I suspect that a child is in danger, I give immediate instructions about either bringing the child to us or taking it to a hospital." The emotion in Rebecca's voice leaves no doubt that an Amish parent would follow her instructions.

She also confronts local medical personnel. Nothing infuriates her more than hearing that a doctor neglected to perform the simple thirty-five dollar test on an Amish baby at birth. When she learns of such cases, she calls and asks for an explanation. "It is their job as medical professionals to urge their patients to take this test, even if the parents might want to save the money. Whenever I hear about someone among us who hesitates to have the test done, I sit them down and tell them the story of my sister's family."

Rebecca does not fear confrontation. In fact, she thrives on it.

◆ ◆ ◆

In addition to her area of expertise, she also has opinions about many other subjects affecting Amish life. And she seeks out forums to state them.

She writes letters to the editor.

Several months before I visited with Rebecca, one of the local newspapers reported the story of a near-fatal mishap for a seventeen-year-old Amish boy. During a hike in the woods, the young man ran against a bush and ended up with a thorn imbedded under his skin. Not recognizing the danger, his mother treated him by removing the thorn and applying an ointment. Several days later he came down with a severe case of lockjaw and was rushed to the hospital near death.

The local journalist who reported the story chose an unfortunate slant. He claimed the problem was caused by the fact that some Amish elect not to go through the normal round of immunizations for their children.

Many non-Amish folks in the local community were upset, and we found ourselves asking such questions as, "Do all of *your* children and young people have current tetanus shots? If you fell into a bush, would you think to get a tetanus shot?" We thought it unfair to position the problem as peculiar to the Amish.

Rebecca was upset for a very different reason.

"I could not believe how that reporter completely missed the point. He had a golden opportunity to inform the public of the need for keeping tetanus shots current. He had a chance to educate. He missed it."

She wrote an articulate, highly charged letter to the editor, which included not one word of defense for her people, but which urged everyone—Amish, as well as non-Amish—to update tetanus shots. She had seized the day. Her opinion was heard.

◆ ◆ ◆

Rebecca also sometimes attends local township meetings.

When an issue comes before a township government which affects them, numerous Amish may attend. However, they seldom speak up during a public meeting.

Several years ago the township where Rebecca lives was struggling with a development question which promised to have a negative impact on several Amish farmers. The media devoured the story. The developers, commissioners, and land preservationists went after each other with a vengeance. The Amish, it seemed to me, were caught in the middle, mere pawns in the struggle.

So I was surprised to open my paper one morning and discover a photo of Rebecca with microphone in hand, addressing the meeting. Fervent in her defense of the preservation of farmland, she pled for the supervisors to carefully consider their decision. The development was denied at the time, but later granted to a different nearby acreage.

I find Rebecca's actions unusual, but, as I sit across from her, I am no longer surprised.

She is independent.

Determined.

Outspoken.

Intense.

◆ ◆ ◆

Those are personality traits, it seems to me, which fit for a person with a high energy, successful career. "Do they fit with being an Amish woman?" is the question I cannot let go.

In my search for an answer, Rebecca and I talk about a difficult-to-understand dynamic in Amish life. On its surface, Amish life thrives because, among other reasons, 1) people are born Amish, and it is difficult to leave; 2) church members learn to submit to the absolute will of the community; and 3) church leaders extend a severe form of punishment—shunning—to those who digress.

Those are facts, ideas, and actions which appear to be the underlying pillars that support life among the Amish. However, a search beneath the surface reveals much more benevolent anchors for this community.

◆ ◆ ◆

Children are encouraged to stay Amish, yes, but they are also given freedom to explore the larger world. Many Amish young people do lots of experimenting during their teen years—they party, they drink and smoke, they learn to enjoy country music, they play guitars and banjoes and drums, they practice bundling, a courtship custom where the young people sleep together without undressing.

Many parents stand by, urging their children to be careful, to consider conforming, and to be faithful. Many other parents are more strict, forbidding their children to participate in the experimentation. A few parents expect the "sowing of some wild oats," as they call it.

Some Amish young folks are lost to the Amish way forever. But many, many more eventually choose to change their ways and settle into long, fruitful years of being Amish. But they have not been coerced; they have made a free choice to be Amish.

◆ ◆ ◆

Neither do members of the Amish church blindly submit to decisions made by the leaders without asking questions. Discussions about what new inventions, ideas, or habits should be permitted to enter community life are constant and involve everyone.

Women talk about them at quiltings and reunions. Men talk about them at barnraisings and haymakings. Husbands consult their wives. Preachers, often influenced by an abundance of freely stated opinions, get together and decide.

Once a decision is made, however, people are expected to conform. Those who decide not to conform or to leave will be confronted by church leaders.

◆ ◆ ◆

To many Amish, the practice of shunning is a painful reminder that they are not perfect. To those of us who are not Amish, it is sometimes a temptation to believe that being Amish must be synonymous with oppression and strictness and lack of choice. It seems to us unlikely, or even impossible, that such a society could produce women like Rebecca.

Indeed, leaving the Amish church is not easy; it is painful; it is often a time of high emotion. In reality, though, it is not that different from leaving any other strong religious community—whether Jewish or Catholic, fundamentalist or southern Baptist. Most wounds heal with time, and those who leave most often rebuild their connections to family members who are still Amish.

Among the Lancaster County Amish, the enforcement of shunning has always been layered with technical details. Few families disown a shunned person. Rather, they remain closely connected and conform to the church's requirements by holding up the letter of the law. For example, they don't sit down at a table with a shunned person, but they will eat at a different table in the same room. They cannot ride in a car driven by the person who has been excommunicated. But they can ride with the shunned person in his or her car as long as someone else drives.

Some Amish question the wisdom of such technicalities and wish the church would reconsider its positions. Many more believe obeying the letter of the law is a way to "keep the peace" and choose, therefore, quietly to adapt.

While the Amish world appears tightly held together, its ability to compromise and negotiate and allow for exceptions is its lifeline. It is filled with people such as Rebecca who are highly self-expressed and who love being Amish.

So it seems to me that oppression, strictness, and lack of choice actually have very little to do with life among the Amish. Most Amish women and men find deep fulfillment in their lives, would not want to live any other way, and frequently find themselves wondering how we people "of the world" can survive with our fragmentation and fragile communities and lack of faith.

◆　◆　◆

I have seen through a small window—through a glass darkly—into this woman's life. Her ability to express her opinions is a vital element of her wholeness, of her complete self. She has learned well how to do that within the confines of Amish life.

Rebecca muses briefly and says, "For me, it fits."

I look around her kitchen. At her furniture. At her mementos. At her decorations. This is certainly a place deeply immersed in Amish society.

Her young nephew walks up onto the front porch, struggling with a garden hose. In the dialect, she asks, what is he trying to do? He responds also in the dialect, *"Ich wills nei wickla fah dich"* (I want to wrap it up for you).

She thanks him, telling him if it's too difficult she can do it later. He accomplishes his feat and goes happily back to his parents' home.

Rebecca's voice quivers and drops several octaves as she looks directly at me, "I love my family, my community, and my church. In my soul, I am probably much more Amish than you might think."

I know that she is right. I am glad to know she loves her world. I am glad to discover that being Amish fits for Rebecca.

CHAPTER NINE

I Am a Shepherdess

Naomi is seventy-eight years old and spry as the frisky lambs in her barn.

An old woman with a young soul, she has weathered well being Amish.

The tidy farmstead, where she lives with her only son and his family, lies in the foothills above the Conestoga Valley. Wildflowers bloom exuberantly on the banks and in the landscaped beds around the house. From her living room window or the fencerow down by the barn, Naomi's vista of the valley expands as it meets the distant horizon.

Distinguished by small villages and dozens of Amish and Mennonite farms, the view offers a perspective of the clouds and sky that rivals the best panorama anywhere in Lancaster County.

◆　◆　◆

When I first spoke to my sister-in-law, Lill, about my quest for Amish stories and Amish roots, she said, "Oh my, you must talk to my Aunt Naomi. What a life she has lived."

So it was that I found myself driving with my niece, two nephews, and their parents—Jon and Lill—through the easternmost part of Lancaster County's Amish community in search of Aunt Naomi's house.

◆ ◆ ◆

We arrive near suppertime on an early June evening, and Naomi meets us at her front door, apologizing that she has not yet had time to feed her sheep. Would we want to join her, she wonders?

Yes, we would!

Skirting a radiant rosebush, several spreading morning glory vines, and beds of flowers in lush bloom, we head for the nearby barn where we are greeted by a herd of bleating sheep. Anxiously awaiting their evening feeding. Anxiously awaiting the touch of this gentle old woman.

Naomi moves easily into the lamb pen with my six-year-old nephew in tow. He wants to pet the lambs and coaxes me to join him. Gingerly, I agree, touching the soft layer of wool on the growing babies while they busily concentrate on the feed which

Naomi pours into the trough.

Vicki. Lori. Sarah. Snowflake. All the sheep have names. With a self-effacing, shy chuckle, Naomi says, "I am a shepherdess." There can be no doubt about that as she murmurs to the lambs and ewes.

"Be careful there, girls.

"Oh, are you that hungry?

"Now you know me, don't you?"

A James Herriot aura envelops the barn as Naomi spins the first of many stories. Pointing to one of the ewes, she says, "I almost lost her this spring. She had four lambies. Four. Can you imagine such a thing?" The ewe had been acting strangely for several days, and Naomi was pretty sure she would have more than the usual twins. But she expected triplets, not quadruplets.

So after assisting the mother through the birth of two lambs, she pulled out what she thought was the third and final lamb. It was dead. Naomi dried off the living babies, put them close to the mother, and went back to the house to take a break. Several hours later she checked on the mother and discovered to her consternation that the ewe was still in labor.

"Are you gonna have another lambie?!" Naomi says she asked the struggling mother.

"That was quite a time. I thought I was losing her. But that fourth lamb came out kicking and baaing. I could not believe it. I have never had quads. I sure wish all four of them had lived.

"For several days it was a big struggle to keep that girl alive. But I bottle-fed the babies and managed to nurse the ewe back to health."

◆ ◆ ◆

All her life Naomi has been a farm woman. She loves animals and has always been surrounded by them. But could she be called an animal lover, I wonder? No, it is not that. Rather, she feels a connection to and regard for all living creatures. But she, like most farmers, also believes that animals were created on a lower level of the food chain than humans.

She points affectionately to one lamb, saying she would not part with her. In the next sentence, she notes the soon departure of most of the other lambs for market. She watches prices, hoping to send them at the best possible time. "Lamb, you know, is a delicacy to many people."

Philip, my ten-year-old nephew, notices that the ewes and her one ram have recently been shorn. He asks how she accomplished that. Naomi explains that she leaves that task to the sheepshearers. It so happens that the shearers had passed through several days earlier, relieving the herd of its wintertime coat and paying her well for the wool.

"No, I don't shear the sheep myself. That would just be too much work for me." With his characteristic sympathetic and understanding look, Philip smiles and nods.

◆ ◆ ◆

Naomi has also invited Lill's parents, David and Rebecca, to join us for the evening meal.

David is Naomi's brother.

Almost immediately after he arrives, David and Naomi embark on a fast track of joking and camaraderie which is for my benefit, but which also holds a mirror to their lives.

As we sit around Naomi's well appointed table, feasting on a mashed potato and ham casserole with a green, garden salad, the children and I listen in awe as their grandfather and his sister tell tales of Amish life in the 1920s and 1930s.

They had to work hard.

Aunt Naomi describes how she operated heavy farm equipment as a very young person. "I was so young that Mother worried. Our father was not well, and someone had to make sure the fieldwork got done. Once Mother timed me when I was mowing hay. She figured out how long it took to make one round in the field. When she thought I should be coming around to where she could see me, she stepped outside and watched to make sure I was still sitting on the mower.

"Actually, I was so young that I had to brace myself with my feet to keep from falling off." Looking at my twelve-year-old niece, Aunt Naomi wonders, "Can you imagine something like that?"

Becky shakes her head no, and all of us, including Naomi, are glad.

"Why I remember having to hitch up the horses when I was so small that I had to stand on a crate. On a crate!"

Naomi says she had a strong constitution, and her mother depended on her. She was not the oldest child. In fact, she came fourth, but she worked beside her older brother as though she herself were a boy.

◆　◆　◆

David, who was much younger, asks Naomi to tell the story about the lame horse. It was the height of the Depression. The family was barely able to keep the farm. Their father was emotionally distraught and unable to function much of the time.

They had an old horse which Naomi rode to harrow the corn. He had a habit of collapsing from exhaustion. So as she rode through the field, she learned to stay alert, ready to leap off before he collapsed. "I could always tell it was about to happen when his ears started to curl up. So I jumped. Then I just had to stand there and wait until he would get back up again."

I try to imagine such a scene and find myself wondering how this woman who was robbed of her childhood with adult responsibilities managed to survive. It could not have been easy.

And may well be the reason why she has a profound reluctance to talk about how it felt. She would rather not think about those times.

I tell her that the stories about her father remind me of some of the stories about my grandfather—Grandmother Mary's husband. Her eyes immediately become several shades brighter as she remembers, "Oh yes, my mother and your Grandmother Mary were cousins. They often would get together and talk about their husbands. They prayed and cried and laughed together many times. I guess it helped them to talk about it. I don't know why my father was that way.

"Mother always used to say to me, 'I sure hope you get a good husband, because you certainly deserve one.' Well, I did."

◆ ◆ ◆

Young adulthood was a much better time for Naomi. Because at least on Sundays she could escape the work. The pain in her eyes brightens into joy as she turns to me and says, "Your other grandmother—Fannie—and I were friends. She was much older than I was, but somehow we just clicked. She took an interest in me. I guess it was because I used to spend so much time at their house on Sundays."

I am surprised and pleased so I ask whether she knew my uncles. "Oh yes, we used to have so much fun with Gid and Jake.

Whenever we played 'Big Four,' I loved when Gid was my partner. He was tall and I was short, and he just used to swing me around." Naomi's arms swing in a warm gesture that evokes youth and barns and banjoes and square dances.

Her voice descends almost to a whisper and she confides, "Why, you know what, I used to wish he would ask me for a date. But he never did. Gid went off to service, and I learned to know Dan. Many years later I told your Grandmother Fannie. She just looked at me and laughed."

Having known my grandmother, I suspect she probably once may have wished the same.

❖ ❖ ❖

In 1935 Naomi married Dan. He had traveled widely before their marriage, and he brought an energy to Naomi's life which is still with her, though he has been gone for sixteen years.

They had two children.

They made their living raising chickens.

Whenever they had a break from the broilers, they traveled. Oh how they traveled! Early in their years together, they always went by train. When their son decided not to be Amish, they went as a family in his car. "We had some very good times together."

She turns pensive as she remembers Dan's dream for when they stopped farming. He had learned to love the railroad and dreamed of taking their grandchildren on a railroad trip to the West Coast, returning by way of southern Canada. Naomi is contemplative and sad as she tells of the debilitating illness which took away that opportunity and eventually also took her beloved Dan.

◆　◆　◆

But she still travels. Her sister Ruth has also been a widow for many years, and they "go every chance we get." The talk about traveling reminds David of another story which he convinces Naomi to tell.

Several summers ago, she and Ruth went to Kansas with Naomi's daughter. They stopped for a day in St. Louis. David interjects to tell me that when Ruth and Naomi get together, they can be quite giddy and silly.

They took the obligatory ride to the top of the Gateway Arch. "We had a good time in those buckets." But the fun really started when they emerged giggling from the arch. Ruth had dared Naomi to try something.

They had been discussing their wrinkles and reminded each other of several biblical stories where folks dipped themselves in water to receive healing. So on an impulse, they decided to wash their faces in the Mississippi River. "Ruth has more wrinkles than I do, but I went with her. Yes, indeed, we went down and washed our faces in that river. It was fun, but we still have wrinkles." Naomi's eyes twinkle, and we all laugh with her.

◆　◆　◆

When I visit Naomi around ten o'clock on a balmy summer morning, she brightly suggests we take a carafe of iced tea and some glasses and walk up to the picnic area.

On the way up the hillside behind her house, she points to an overgrowth of vines, small trees, and brush and remarks that the neatly mown area we are approaching once looked like that.

After Dan died, Naomi's children wished she lived closer to them. So she and her son found the now palatial ten-acre farmstead. "But you should have seen it. It was all grown up, and so much work for the first years."

Naomi moved onto the property first. One Sunday afternoon she decided to take a walk around the land to see how many different species of wildflowers she could find. "You know, I found sixty different kinds, and I knew then that this place would be beautiful someday."

She decided to surprise the family by clearing off a large plot in the woods. Gradually she hacked away at the growth, eventually creating this refuge. "I often come up here when I want to be alone. It is so peaceful." In fact, the only sounds come from chirping birds in the trees and croaking bullfrogs in the small natural pond which appeared as she worked at clearing the land.

A picnic table and small grilling area complete the restful scene. "Our whole family camped up here on the Fourth of July. We had such a good time."

I look across the table at this resilient woman. I know her good friend—my grandmother Fannie—would be glad to know so much of Naomi's life had gone well. Would be glad to know the young woman in whom she took a special interest, the middle-aged woman to whom she wrote many letters, had grown into this gracious old person. A person, I think to myself, not unlike Fannie herself.

CHAPTER TEN

Of Mountain Homes and Amish Ways

I have always known Katie to be a warm and social woman. When her daughter and I arrive soon after 8:30 on a Thursday morning in July, she is quickly trying to finish her weekly cleaning. But she dries her hands, gives her daughter an affectionate kiss, throws her arms around me, and says, "Oh my, Louise, it's been a long time since I saw you."

She loves to be with people. I have come to see her because I am curious to know how she has survived the move from her Lancaster County home to this fledgling Amish settlement in the mountains of central Pennsylvania.

How she has rebuilt her life.

How she has adjusted to the differences.

How she has connected to this new place.

I am also eager to hear why she and her husband, Jake, decided to leave Lancaster County—the place where they were born and raised, where they married, where they raised their family.

◆　◆　◆

Their oldest daughter Marianne, who has come with me to visit her parents, is married to my brother Amos. I remember how surprised we all were to hear Marianne say, "Dad and Mom sold the farm."

It was unexpected. Katie and Jake leaving Lancaster County? Katie was fifty-three; Jake was almost sixty. They were ready for a break from the sunrise to sunset toil of a family farm. Their six children each had busy lives of their own; none were in a position to take over the homestead.

Jake especially wanted to leave the farm, but he also wanted the land to stay in Amish hands. So he spread the word. "Before I was ready, people were knocking on our door, asking to buy," Katie tells me. They sold at a fair price to an Amish neighbor. And moved to Perry County's Sherman Valley, about an hour and a half by car from the heart of the Lancaster Amish settlement.

◆　◆　◆

The first Amish came to the Sherman Valley in 1977. For nearly ten years, the settlement barely survived with only the three original families. Those folks, Katie remembers, made many trips (by hired van driver) back to Lancaster—for weddings, family reunions, funerals, and young folks get-togethers.

Then in the mid-1980s, other Lancaster Amish discovered Perry County, and the area's Amish population suddenly grew faster than the corn and beans on the farms some of them were buying. Katie and Jake arrived in 1989. Today more than fifty Amish families live within no more than a few miles of Route 17, the highway which bisects the valley. Three one-room schools, built in the typical Lancaster Amish style, now stand empty, silently awaiting late August and the return of teachers and students eager to learn and grow. From Ickesburg to Blain to New Germantown, Amish farms and businesses dot the valley.

Katie tells me that only about half of the Amish in Perry County are farmers. Others have set up businesses, reflecting the changing climate of Amish life. There is a stone mason. A contractor and builder. A proprietor of a meat market stand at Harrisburg's Broad Street farmers' market.

I realize that her descriptions of life among the Amish of Perry County sound almost identical to the descriptions I have heard of Lancaster County. Their leaving Lancaster has not significantly changed their lives. The Perry County Amish have not recaptured a past way of Amish living. They have not all become farmers again. They have not solved all of their problems. They have not resorted to fewer contacts with the larger world. So why did they leave Lancaster?

◆　◆　◆

Why did Katie and Jake leave Lancaster? I ask her.

"Jake always said he wanted a mountain home. We really like the peace and quiet, the slower pace of life. We also came for the nature."

They love the mountains. Katie points out her kitchen window and says, "Just before you came there were four doe up there at the feeder. I was so wishing you could have seen them." She turns and points out the window on the other side of her kitchen and remarks at the many species of birds—hummingbirds, chickadees, goldfinches, cardinals, and woodpeckers—who come to feast at one of the largest bird feeders I have ever seen.

They love their view of the valley. The home they bought hugs the valley's northwest ridge and looks down over lush farmland toward Route 17. As we sip coffee in the front lawn, which is actually an embankment on the side of the mountain, Katie talks about life among the neighbors in Perry County.

She and Jake also love the people. "Everyone is so friendly. Why the first Sunday morning when we went to church, people passed us in their cars and waved. We could not believe it." As we visit, Katie talks about her new friends. The Amish widow who is building a house on her family farm at the foot of the mountain just below Jake and Katie's house. The woman in nearby Blain who visits Katie at least once a week. The neighbor just on the other side of Katie's long lane who owns the restaurant over in New Germantown.

"We fell in love with this place when we visited Sam and Naomi," Katie offers as another reason for their move. Naomi is one of her daughters, and she and Sam with their preschool children moved to the valley a year or two before Jake and Katie. They live within easy walking distance on a trail across the densely wooded mountainside.

◆　◆　◆

To me, Jake and Katie's reasons for leaving Lancaster County sound much like the explanations most people give for moving from place to place.

A desire for new experiences.

For a change of pace.

For adventure.

And I wonder how her simple answer meshes with the ongoing debate and the sometimes irrational predictions about the effects of the world on Lancaster County's Amish society.

Tourism.

Encroaching technology.

Undisciplined development.

Those are the reasons most often cited for what some people believe will be the end of Amish life in southeastern Pennsylvania. Experts and opinion makers, statisticians and sociologists, Amish and non-Amish all sometimes align themselves along a path of doom which predicts the final chapter for the Amish of Lancaster County. They will all eventually leave, it is claimed.

There is just too much commercialization.

Too much contact with the world.

Too much pressure to be modern.

◆　◆　◆

I am interested. I am sad. I am hopeful. Katie tells me a story. Recently when she spent a day with some of her sisters and other friends in the Lancaster area, she heard about a young family who really wanted to move "to one of the valleys." (This is how the Amish speak of the numerous central Pennsylvania Amish settlements such as the one in Perry County.) But the young woman's parents pled with them not to leave. They decided to stay.

Katie thought that strange, saying, "Why they wouldn't be that far away. They could still see them often. It's not like they wanted to move to Indiana or Kentucky or Florida." And she exchanged a knowing look with Marianne.

Some years earlier Amos and Marianne had moved to Sarasota with their preschool sons, always a point of sadness for Katie. While she visited them in Florida as often as she could, she missed growing up with those grandsons and sometimes wished they were closer. When Amos and Marianne returned to Lancaster County some years later, Katie was glad. But then she and Jake left. I find in her story a reflection of the ambivalence many Amish feel about leaving familiar surroundings, family and friends, hearth and home.

"This is our home. Why would we want to leave?" one woman asserted when I asked whether she thought the Amish might all one day leave Lancaster County. Many Amish parents urgently keep their children close, subdividing their farms over and over again and establishing ingenious cottage industries—a woodworking shop, a farm equipment business, a health food store—to ensure an income for everyone. Others find traveling to other valleys fun and are pleased to see their children branching out. Others, such as Katie and Jake, decide to try the adventure themselves.

I find myself wondering, therefore, if Amish migration does not have much more to do with the spirit of pioneering, the opportunity for change, and the appeal of new geography than it has to do with development, tourism, and technology. Certainly that can be said about Jake and Katie.

◆　◆　◆

Their move to Perry County had few, if any, connections to the development of Lancaster farmland. When they decided to sell their farm, there was never any question to whom they should sell. An Amish farmer, of course. Jake would never for one moment have entertained the thought of getting rich off his land. Marianne jumps in with a story about her father.

Soon after the move to Perry, Jake took a job with a building contractor. After several years of work, his boss gave him a raise. Jake refused the money, saying, "We don't need it." Marianne shakes her head with obvious respect and pride, "I don't know if I have ever in my life heard of such a thing." Katie interjects, "That's just how Jake is." We all recognize the Amish way in Jake's actions.

♦ ♦ ♦

Neither did Jake and Katie's move to Perry County disconnect them from the effects of tourism. Several years ago, they began thinking about a source of income for Jake so he would not need to work away from home. Having spent his entire life farming, he realized how much he enjoyed being at home. He took an interest in the production of Amish straw hats, got some tips from the two women who make most of the hats worn by Lancaster County Amish, bought a sewing machine, and laboriously taught himself the trade.

Claiming his early attempts were downright comical, Katie produces several oddly shaped hats as proof. Her mirth, mingled with pride over his accomplishment, peppers our conversation for the next several hours. She talks about how the buzzing of the machine drove her crazy "and he had nothing to show for it." She describes how they moved the sewing machine from the house to a room on the second floor of their small horse barn. She invites us to go with her to the barn where we find Jake busily producing woven wheat straw hats. "It takes him about forty-five minutes to do one hat, depending on its size."

The woven straw, which is kept moist in a pan of water, responds to Jake's fingers as he guides it into the shape of a hat. We watch over his shoulders as Katie describes the process and the people who wear the hats.

Amish men and boys all over Perry County.

The banker in the nearby village of Blain.

A neighbor who asked for an extra-wide brim.

"Half of Blain wears Jake's hats," Katie declares with an "I-can't-believe-it" chuckle. Some of the hats also eventually come into the hands of Lancaster County tourists, thanks to several craft shops back home who buy "all he can make." In fact, business is booming and Jake finds it difficult to keep up with the demand.

"I guess maybe I'll have to learn how to do it too," Katie says.

◆ ◆ ◆

Just as Jake and Katie's move to Perry County did not disconnect them from tourism, it also did not disconnect them from the questions about technology which consistently cause debate in Amish society. The geography of Perry County accounts for fewer people and greater isolation. Early on, most Amish who came to the valley argued that telephones were important communication links and should be permitted. Most people installed one inside their homes.

The recent ballooning of the Amish population brought new blood, along with old ideas and a significant group who wished to stay closer to "the old Amish ways." The church opted to keep peace by asking members to remove the phones from their homes, deciding it was fine to keep the telephones on the properties as long as they were far enough away so they could not be used on a whim.

Jake and Katie moved their phone into a shed a short distance from the house. And they know it will surely not be the last time the church needs to "draw the line" on some question of technology.

◆ ◆ ◆

The conversation turns to Katie's job. For more than fifteen years she has been "standing on market" at least one day a week. From the widely known Central Market in the city of Lancaster to Philadelphia's Reading Terminal Market to lesser known markets in Baltimore, Reading, and Harrisburg, Amish women have been standing at farmers' market stalls, selling produce and flowers and crafts for decades. Sometimes the stands are owned by other Amish folks, but the "market women" also work for non-Amish proprietors.

Every Friday Katie gets up at 4:30 in order to be ready when the van arrives. A member of her church operates a meat market stand at the Harrisburg market and employs a local van driver to make the weekly trip.

Katie works at the Auntie Anne soft pretzel stand. "I love my job because I can talk to people." I ask whether it is a chance for her to see old friends from Lancaster who also attend this market. She nods.

Marianne smiles and reminds her, "But Mom, you know, it's mostly because you like to talk to the customers."

"We do have lots of regular customers, and I get to know them. I stand out front and roll pretzels so I can see everyone who comes up." I can easily picture this broad, self-assured, and congenial woman making lots of connections with the weary office workers and city shoppers who stop by for one of the famous baked soft pretzels.

A sheepish grin is followed with the confession, "Sometimes I have to be careful that I keep up with rolling pretzels."

◆　◆　◆

I am anxious to see more of Perry County, and Marianne wants to stop by and see Naomi and the children. So Katie informs Jake he will need to make his own lunch, and we women drive down the mountain and southwest on Route 17 toward Blain. Along the way, Katie frequently points to a farm or perhaps a smaller house and says, "That's an Amish place."

She recommends the restaurant in New Germantown which is owned by Pat, the neighbor who has become her close friend. It is a delightful country restaurant in the middle of nowhere with a great view of the Sherman Valley.

Katie tells the story about how she convinced Pat to use a homemade sauce on her steak sandwiches instead of the canned pizza sauce. "The first time I had Pat's pizza steaks, I told her about my steak sauce recipe. She asked for it, and whenever she has time she makes some and puts it on the menu. That homemade sauce makes delicious steak sandwiches."

Because Katie's recipe isn't on the menu, we settle for hot roast beef sandwiches and french fries with iced tea. The restaurant is busy, but Pat soon comes out from the kitchen and sits down beside Katie.

Vast cultural differences separate these two women. But they have become great friends, and a warmth flows between them as they catch up on neighborhood gossip. Pat's battle with glaucoma draws a characteristic murmur of care and concern from Katie.

Katie is an Amish woman, immersed in Amish ways. She is also a faithful and loyal friend. It is obvious that the circumstances of her life have not changed her ways.

CHAPTER ELEVEN

I Am Glad to Have Been Amish

I am glad once to have been Amish. Glad to have been among women such as Mary and Fannie and Susie and Katie and Naomi. Glad to have grown up in the warmth of their embrace. Glad to have been marked and matured by their lives and their inspirations.

It is a simple life, with simple rhythms—the life of an Amish woman. A place where gardens and flowers, fields and clover, children and home determine routine.

It is a quiet life, with quiet hopes—the life of an Amish woman. A place where reading and writing, quilting and sewing, cooking and cleaning consume most of time.

It is a worker's life, marked by the features of a working woman. A place where broad shoulders and large hands and strong arms and sturdy backs are beautiful.

It is a religious life, marked by the features of a religious woman.

A place where head coverings and uniform styles and Bibles and hymn books are lovely.

It is a life I still sometimes long for. One I do not have—nor ever will have—but one which I treasure and from which I have learned much. In both its transcendent benevolence, and its broken shards.

For it is not utopian. It is touched by grief and loss. By pain and misunderstanding. By buried hopes and hopeless dreams.

But it is also touched by joy and fortune. By pleasure and appreciation. By living hopes and hopeful dreams.

◆ ◆ ◆

In my quest to understand what it meant to be an Amish woman, I chose not to limit my connections only to those women I knew to be especially gifted or particularly successful. There are many such women among the Amish.

One who spent years providing assistance to reseachers at Johns Hopkins University. One who frequently takes continuing education classes and is known among the professors and students of a local seminary as an able theologian. One who is a skilled entrepreneur and has been her family's primary breadwinner throughout the thirty-some years of her marriage. All of these women are also thoroughly Amish. But they could not be considered typical or ordinary.

I decided to seek out ordinary people. Women who live in quiet homes and on secluded farmsteads, far away from the rush and hurry of late twentieth century life.

In the ordinariness of their lives, I encountered extraordinary gifts and grace. Homemakers. Mothers. Quilters. Artists. Lovers of C.S. Lewis. Lovers of children. Farmers. Writers. Career women. And, most of all, women who are loyal and faithful friends. There are many thousands of Amish women such as these.

They are warm.

And gracious.

And strong.

And sure.

◆　◆　◆

Among these ordinary women, I found hope for the future. For they do not seek answers to post-modern dilemmas. They only seek opportunities to make a difference in their small worlds. They do not seek freedom. They only seek chances to exercise free will within the confines of their responsibilities to the community.

Some preferred not to talk to me. Several months after one such woman said no, she would rather not, I met her again at a large gathering. She received me with her characteristic warmth and jollity and reminded me that she just would not have had enough of interest to share. But the postcard which I sent, expressing my thanks for her forthrightness, she told me, was still on her refrigerator.

Like this woman who said no, the women with whom I spoke offered me acceptance. They did not always understand me, but they listened to my stories. And they freely shared stories of their own.

◆　◆　◆

These are the women of my story.

They are daughters. And sisters. And wives. And mothers. But, most of all, they are Amish women with the indelible marks of Amish ways and understandings imprinted on their mannerisms, their styles, and their grace.

About the Author

Louise Stoltzfus was born and raised in a Lancaster County Amish family. She is the author of *Two Amish Folk Artists: The Story of Henry Lapp and Barbara Ebersol.*

Stoltzfus is an editor for Good Books and has co-authored four cookbooks—*The Central Market Cookbook, The Best of Mennonite Fellowship Meals, Favorite Recipes from Quilters,* and *Lancaster County Cookbook.* She is also director of The People's Place Gallery, Intercourse, Pennsylvania, and lives in Lancaster, Pennsylvania, ten miles from her ancestral home.